*R*outes of
Cross-Cultural
Exchange

Trans-Saharan Trade Routes

Matt Lang

Cavendish
Square

New York

Published in 2018 by Cavendish Square Publishing, LLC
243 5th Avenue, Suite 136, New York, NY 10016

Website: cavendishsq.com

CPSIA Compliance Information: Batch #CS17CSQ

Library of Congress Cataloging-in-Publication Data

Names: Lang, Matt, author.
Title: Trans-Saharan trade routes / Matt Lang.
Other titles: Routes of cross-cultural exchange.
Description: New York : Cavendish Square Publishing, 2018. | Series: Routes of cross-cultural exchange | Includes bibliographical references and index.
Identifiers: LCCN 2016051047 (print) | LCCN 2016051503 (ebook) | ISBN 9781502628596 (library bound) | ISBN 9781502628602 (E-book)
Subjects: LCSH: Trade routes--Sahara. | Sahara--Civilization. | Sahara--Commerce--History.
Classification: LCC DT337 .L36 2017 (print) | LCC DT337 (ebook) | DDC 966--dc23
LC record available at https://lccn.loc.gov/2016051047

Editorial Director: David McNamara
Editor: Caitlyn Miller
Copy Editor: Alex Tessman
Associate Art Director: Amy Greenan
Designer: Jessica Nevins
Production Coordinator: Karol Szymczuk
Photo Research: J8 Media

Table of Contents

The Desert Highway

Timbuktu has a reputation as being a faraway place, and it is. Timbuktu is a city in the West African country of Mali, just on the southern edge of the Sahara Desert near a bend in the Niger River. These days it is surrounded and partially covered by sand, but it was once surrounded by forests. Over 54,000 people live there today, though it once had a population of over 100,000 or more, depending on the season. Now there is one paved road leading from the center of the town out to the airport. There are other roads in and around the city, but they, too, are covered in sand. While the modern city is poor and isolated, at the height of its glory (in the 1400s) it was arguably the most important stop on an extensive trade network. That network spanned across the Sahara Desert, from the forests of West Africa north to the Mediterranean Sea; and east to Egypt and what is now Ethiopia.

During every election and during every political debate, candidates, politicians, and economists talk about trade. Individual people trade with one another, and groups of people trade with each other. Today, the United States trades with Canada,

The Sahara Desert

Mexico, Japan, China, and many other countries. Countries trade raw materials like oil, cobalt, and magnesium. Manufactured products like cars, computers, and cell phones are important imports and exports. And people trade food like rice, corn, and beef. They might even trade one kind of currency for another.

Though trade looks different now than it did twenty, fifty, or one hundred years ago, trade is not new. People have been trading with each other from the very beginning of human history. Trade is one of many powerful forces that has helped shaped civilization as we know it, because when goods are exchanged, so are ideas.

When people trade goods, they also learn about each other's languages, customs, and traditions. Trade partners have to communicate with each other, so they begin learning, at least to a certain extent, one another's language. One group may even begin using new words or phrases in their own language. As different groups trade with each other, they may be invited to participate in different important ceremonies and customs. Other people may even fall in love and get married. All of these circumstances foster the exchange of ideas and values. Trade even shapes where people live. People who used to live in villages may move into cities, people who used to live on the coast may move inland, and people who used to be farmers may become merchants. Nomads may become sedentary, and practitioners of one religion may decide to practice another.

The trans-Saharan trade routes were no different from the trade routes of today in that they involved a transfer of goods and ideas. However, modern trade is done by planes, trains, boats, and even electronic transfer. Alternatively, trans-Saharan trade was done mostly by **caravans** of camels.

The Sahara Desert is the largest hot desert in the world, stretching across most of Northern Africa. It is 2,983 miles (4,800 kilometers) long, 1,118 miles (1,799 kilometers) wide. The desert covers a total area of 3,629,360 square miles (9,399,999 square kilometers), making it almost as large as the United States. People have lived in the Sahara Desert and traded with each other since ancient times, but the peak of the trans-Sahara trade routes was from the eighth century to the early seventeenth century.

Many different groups established the trans-Saharan trade routes, such as the Mande (including the Malinke and Soninke), Berbers (including the Zanata, Sanhaja, and Tuareg), Arabs, Fulani, Songhai, and others. Some, like the Berbers, have lived in parts of Northern Africa for at least ten thousand years. Others, like the Arabs, arrived more recently in the seventh century. All played a role along the trade routes and were influenced in different ways by other groups. The Arabs had the most influence, bringing with them their language, alphabet, and their religion (Islam), though they were also influenced by local groups. To this day, Islam is practiced across North and West Africa. Yet it looks different in different places, and it changed as life along the trade routes changed.

The following chapters look at the climate of the Sahara and the challenges and opportunities that come from living in that region. You'll learn about the different kinds of people who lived there: where they lived, how they lived, the languages they spoke, and the religions and customs they practiced. We'll also look at what life was like before the trade route compared to what life was like after the trade route became established. Finally, we'll discuss what happened to the trade route. You'll learn about why and how it came to an end, as well as what life is like along the old trade routes today.

Chapter 1

The Sahara as a Barrier

The Sahara is the world's largest hot desert (the Artic and Antarctica are larger, and technically deserts because they are so dry, but they are not hot). Covering most of North Africa, the modern-day countries of Morocco, Tunisia, Algeria, and Libya, the Sahara extends from the Mediterranean Sea east to the Nile River Valley and south the grasslands known as the **Sahel**. During the time of the trans-Saharan trade routes, the southern part of the Sahara was called the **Sudan** (not to be confused with the present-day country of the same name). Between the coast and the Sudan was the central region known as the **Maghreb**. The trade routes, therefore, went across the Sahara from North Africa, through the Maghreb and Sudan, to the Sahel.

The desert has plenty of sand, of course, but the Sahara also has rocks, mountains, and some rivers.

Opposite: *Pockets of water sustain life in the desert.*

Every so often, there is an area where water pools from a source underground. Even in ancient times, people were able to live in these oases because there was enough water. Therefore, villages were scattered across the Sahara.

Early Civilizations

We don't know exactly what the first human communities in the Sahara were like, since they existed in pre-historic times. But we do know that before the start of the trans-Saharan trade routes, people lived in urban areas along the coast. They also lived farther inland near the rivers, where the climate was better for growing food and where there was better access to transportation. Even though the towns along the coast and the rivers had many people living in them, these people had little contact with each other. The only way to reach each other was by crossing the desert, and this was a very difficult journey.

We also know that the way of life of the early humans changed as the climate in the desert changed. There was a wet phase from 2500 BCE to 300 BCE and an arid phase from 300 BCE to 300 CE. Another wet phase took place from 300 CE to 1100 CE, and yet another dry phase from 100 CE to 1500 CE. When the desert was wet, settlements grew because they could produce more food. Even though travel was easier in the wet phases, because there was more water and the desert was less harsh, people didn't feel the need to travel. This was because they were able to grow enough food close to home.

Travel in the Sahara

Since traveling in the Sahara was so difficult, people only traded if they absolutely needed something and if they knew that they had the ability to make the trip. As the climate in the Sahara changed from wet to dry, villages shrank in size and became more isolated. The isolated communities could no longer provide for themselves, so they needed to find trade partners.

For example, in the southern Sahara, farmers in the grasslands of the Sahel began to trade with cattle-herders farther north in the Sudan. The farmers needed to trade because the climate in the grasslands was too wet for cattle. Any cattle that stayed there for too long would get sick. The cattle-herders in the Sudan needed to trade because the climate in the desert was too dry to grow grains. The farmers had extra grain; the herders had extra cattle. They didn't live too far away from each other, so they traded with each other: milk

Cattle graze on the grasslands of the savannah.

Egypt

In the era before trans-Saharan trade, Egypt was a wealthy civilization that bordered the Sahara to the east. Egypt certainly had plenty of resources to trade and plenty of needs given the number of people who lived there. Egypt was located along the sea coast, but the Egyptians were not great sailors. They conducted some trade using the Red Sea, but nothing that came close to reaching the other

Ancient Egyptians didn't use roads, they used boats to trade along the Nile instead. The Nile allowed Egyptians to move goods from the coast to the interior.

side of the Sahara. The Egyptians also chose not to venture into the desert to the west. They gave the desert the name "Maghreb," meaning *west,* and they felt that the Maghreb was a wild place that was best avoided. Egypt did, however, trade along the Nile River, with communities farther south. The wealthier towns, cities, and civilizations, like Egypt, could produce food for communities in the desert. It might seem that the people in the desert had little to offer the people on the coast and near the rivers. Yet one of the most important resources found in the desert was salt. Farmers worked all

day in the hot sun; as they worked, they would sweat and become dehydrated. Because the only place to get salt was in the desert and salt is an important way of rehydrating, desert communities held a valuable resource. Sadly, another desert resource was people. Slaves were also traded from towns in the interior to labor in the farms and cities near the coast and rivers.

The Egyptians would travel south along the Nile, which took them as far as modern-day Sudan. Once it reached that point, the river became too difficult to travel, so donkey caravans were used to move goods and people the rest of the way. Donkeys were useful for taking short trips and were only used in local trade. They were not part of the trans-Saharan trade routes.

and cattle in exchange for grains. But this was local trade, not *trans*-Saharan trade.

There were also large and wealthy towns such as Djenné in the Empire of Mali (which is not the same as the modern nation of Mali) that were successful because they were built along a river. In this case the town was along the Niger River, which meant Djenné had water for crops and could use the river for transportation. The Niger River was useful for local trade, but it was full of rapids, and boats couldn't travel on it for long distances. Therefore, it was not helpful in establishing a trans-Saharan trade route.

The Berbers

After the desert dried, settlements in the interior shrank in size as people moved to the grasslands farther south. Berber-speaking people from near the Mediterranean began moving into the Sahara. The Berbers were able to navigate the desert with the help of horses. Before long, they became the dominant group in the Sahara, and they were well positioned to play a key role in the creation of the trans-Saharan trade routes.

The Berbers built kingdoms in the interior, and these kingdoms were powerful enough to form rivalries and alliances with the Romans, who conquered the coastal city of Carthage in 146 BCE. The Romans brought Christianity with them. Some Berbers chose to follow the religion, although the Berber Christians did not necessarily want to follow the rules of Rome. The religious differences, along with Berber resistance to Roman taxes and other forms of exploitation such as slavery, led to a series of revolts and other unrest. This unrest was another obstacle to the establishment of long distance trade routes across the Sahara.

There were plenty of active and wealthy civilizations in and around the Sahara. And although there was need for food, cattle, minerals, and labor, most of the trade in the Sahara was local. It would take a new group of people, with both the means and the motivation, to establish trade routes. That new group was the Arabs, who came from the Arabian Peninsula. They came with powerful armies and a new religion, a religion they hoped to spread far and wide: Islam.

Chapter 2

Establishing the Trade Routes

n the seventh century, on the Arabian Peninsula in what is now Saudi Arabia, a man named Muhammad began to visit a cave on a mountain. On one of his trips, he heard what he believed to be the words of God, or *Allah*, speaking to him. Muhammad wrote these words down, and they became the foundation of Islam. Part of this new belief was the conviction that the tribes of Arabia and the people of the world should be united under this one religion. The leaders of the different tribes did not like this challenge to their authority, so they threatened Muhammad and his followers. In 622, Muhammad was forced to flee his home in Mecca. Hundreds of other people fled with him to Medina. It was there that Muhammad first organized his new followers, who came to be called Muslims. Once organized politically, the Muslims were soon ruling the city.

Opposite: *A camel, ready to travel*

The Arrival of Arabs in North Africa

From there, Islam spread, uniting different Arabic speaking tribes under one religion. By the time Muhammad died in 632, almost all of Arabia was under his control. His followers went on to conquer Armenia, Persia, Syria, Palestine, Iraq, and North Africa. They even made it through Spain all the way to France before they were finally defeated. Along the way, they played a vital role in establishing the trans-Saharan trade route.

When Muslims armies first arrived in North Africa, they found a region in the middle of much conflict and turmoil. At first, they did little to bring order, mostly conducting raids to steal goods and slaves. They weren't trying to established a new system of government—yet. The Arabs fought battles with both the Byzantines and Berbers. By the time they defeated the Byzantines, the Arab Muslims had converted many of the local Berbers to Islam. Both Arab Muslims and local Berber converts pushed into the desert. From Egypt, they pushed west into the Maghreb, the desert wilderness that the Egyptians had always avoided. They moved into the Maghreb in 643, where they immediately encountered resistance from the Berbers at large.

The first great hero of the Arab conquest was named Uqba ibn Nafi. Much of his life story is probably more legendary than factual. However, historians believe that he conquered his way through North Africa between 666 to 683, eventually making it as far as present day southern Niger. Ibn Nafi also built a new capital called Qayrawan in the interior of what is now Tunisia. Building a new capital signaled that he was not content to simply raid the area and move away. He wanted a more permanent presence.

Arabs, Berbers, and Trade Routes

While there was new energy directed to the interior, Muslims put most of their energy into conquering along the coast. They were successful, eventually making it all the way into Spain. This was even more notable because most of the Muslims that crossed the Strait of Gibraltar into Spain were Berber. In fact, Gibraltar was named after Tariq ibn Ziyad. Gibraltar is a variation of Jebel Tariq, or "The Mountain of Tariq." Even though there was conflict between Arabs and Berbers in many places, the conquest of Spain also showed that Arabs and Berbers were mostly working together and merging into a powerful new Islamic society.

When the Romans took over Carthage and established themselves as a power in North Africa, many Berbers chose to follow the Romans' religion, Christianity. However, as previously mentioned, the Berbers did not always follow the same style of Christianity as the Romans. Many Berber Christians were Donatists, and they were opposed to the Catholics from Rome. Also, Berbers resisted the heavy taxes the Romans imposed. When the Arabs arrived and brought Islam with them, many Berbers chose to follow the new religion. Yet the Berbers observed Islam in a way that was unique to them.

Ironically, the Berber resistance to orthodox Islam helped to establish the trade routes. Two of the main

Berber sects of Islam were the Ibadis and the Sufris. These sects were made up primarily of merchants who had commercial interest in developing more effective trade in the region. Orthodox Muslims were discouraged, or even prohibited, from interacting with and trading with non-Muslims. But non-Orthodox Muslims did not have to follow such rules. They were free to trade with whomever they wanted. The Ibadis moved farther and farther inland, making alliances with some of the stronger non-Muslim Berber tribes as they went. Then the Ibadis started to trade with these tribes. The Ibadis expanded all the way to southern Algeria, where their territory met with the territory of the Sufris. The Sufris had also been establishing trade partners and routes as they expanded across the desert. By coming together, the Ibadis and the Sufris established the first trade routes that spanned across the whole of the Sahara.

The Kingdoms of the Sahel

On the southern edge of the desert, there were great kingdoms that were remote and unknown in much of the world. Even today, not much is known about these ancient African civilizations. Europeans and Middle Easterners heard stories about the riches that could supposedly be found there. Stories told of shining cities of gold. People even spoke of towers of gold rising out of the desert sand. Of course, these stories were more legends than facts, but there was some truth behind them. There were great and wealthy civilizations south of the Sahara. The oldest and one of the most powerful was Ghana. The modern-day country of Ghana is named after this ancient kingdom

The Camel

Even with the energy and ambition of the Arabs, trans-Saharan trade would not have been possible without another key ingredient: the camel. Because the desert is so sandy and rocky, and since roads as we know them had not been built yet, wheels were of no use when it came to moving things. There is some evidence that wagons and chariots were used in special ceremonies to parade people around. But they were not used to move a large amount of goods over long distances. Horses were helpful for carrying people and some supplies but could not carry enough supplies to make them effective for long distance trade. Oxen were able to carry heavy loads. However, they could not move very fast, so long trips took too much time to be worthwhile.

Camels were introduced from the Middle East and had been in the region as early as 3000 BCE. Like much of the early history of civilization in North Africa, we don't know exactly when camels began to be used to transport goods. We do know they were being used along the Mediterranean in Egypt and in the interior by the Berbers by 100 BCE.

Camels are perfectly adapted to the desert. They are able to withstand large changes in body temperature and can go longer periods of time without water. Camels can absorb water so efficiently that they can sometimes get all the water they need by eating plants. Since camels don't need much water, camel caravans don't need to carry as much water with them. This leaves more space for carrying valuable goods, making camels perfect for use in trans-Saharan trade.

but is located far south of where the kingdom used
to be.

Old Ghana

The earliest written account of Old Ghana comes from
the eighth century. The kingdom reached the height
of its power in the tenth century to claim an area that
now covers the countries of Mali, Mauritania, and
Senegal. Old Ghana got most of its wealth from gold.
In fact, it was sometimes called Golden Ghana, due to
its large storehouses of the precious metal. The gold
made it an attractive destination for Muslim merchants
crossing the desert.

Northwest of Old Ghana, in the desert frontier
around the ninth century, groups of nomadic Berbers
began to work together in a loose federation known
as the Sanhajah. This new federation soon started to
control the trade routes of the western Sahara. By the
eleventh century, the Sanhajah began to follow a very
strict form of Islam. This development came after one
of their chiefs traveled to Mecca and returned with a
scholar, Abd-Allah Ibn Yasin.

Yasin's followers used force to spread his ideas.
They considered their fight *jihad*, or holy war, and the
spirit of jihad united the tribes of the Sanhajah with
a new purpose. In the middle of the eleventh century,
they launched attacks on settlements to the north, and
on the kingdom of Ghana to the south. By 1076, they
were the new occupiers of the Old Ghana. Their rule
lasted for twenty years, after which time the kingdom
began to break apart.

Timbuktu (or Tombuctou) was an important city in the fourteenth century.

Mali

The glory of Old Ghana gave way to a new power: Mali. Mali was formed from pieces of the Old Ghanian empire, as well as from territory in Morocco and surrounding regions. The rulers of the new Islamic Empire of Mali wanted to expand their territory as rulers so often do. They developed new trade routes to new goldfields closer to the Atlantic Ocean. They expanded east to commercial centers like Timbuktu and Gao. And they started to send caravans filled with gold as far away as Egypt.

In 1326, **Mansa** Musa made his pilgrimage to Mecca. All Muslims are expected to make a pilgrimage to Mecca at least once in their lifetime, if they are able. Therefore, the trip itself was not noteworthy. What was noteworthy was the large caravan that accompanied him, hundreds of camels carrying gold. The wealth was impressive, and the trip was also proof that it was possible to cross the Sahara. Furthermore, it proved there were riches to be found on the other side of the desert.

Songhai

South of Mali was another ancient kingdom called Songhai. The origins of this kingdom are mysterious, like so much of the ancient world. The first king we know about was named Za-Kasi, who came to power in the eleventh century CE. He was said to be the first Muslim ruler of Songhai. By the fifteenth century, a ruler named Sonni Ali came to power. Sonni Ali wanted the people to return to their old religion. He began attacking Mali, destroying several cities, and eventually capturing Gao.

After Sonni Ali died in 1492, the new ruler, Al-Hajj Mohammed A'skia, was a Muslim. He re-established Islam as the religion of the kingdom. By most accounts, he ruled peacefully and justly. A'skia also made the pilgrimage to Mecca, further developing economic and political relationships along that route. The ruler even founded a charity in Mecca to support the people of his hometown, Tekrur.

A'skia stepped down from the throne in 1528. In 1591, Songhai was attacked by Morocco, partly to regain control of valuable salt mines. Four thousand soldiers, many of them from Spain, marched under the orders of Sultan Abu Yusuf Ya'qub al-Mansur. They crossed the Sahara and conquered the cities of Gao, Timbuktu, and Djenné. The sultan was never able to rule the areas his army had conquered, however, and Songhai fell into the control of Tuareg nomads. With the collapse of the Songhai, the age of the great kingdoms of West Africa came to an end. But they had made a lasting impacting on the economy of Sahara.

Kanem-Bornu

Farther to the east, around Lake Chad, was the kingdom of Kanem-Bornu. The kingdom lasted from the ninth to the nineteenth century and was famous far and wide. Just like the kingdoms of the west, Kanem-Bornu was so wealthy that stories of its riches reached Europe. At the height of its power, it controlled trans-Saharan caravan traffic from Lake Chad to the Fezzan region in Libya.

Originally, Kanem got its wealth from salt, which was mined a few hundred miles to the north. Its location made it an ideal point for other kinds of trade as well, namely horses, copper, cotton, and slaves. The wealth and influence of Kanem eventually drew the attention of Muslim merchants. Soon Islam became the religion of the kingdom. Kanem took full control of the Fezzan before too long and increased its contact with Cairo and Tunis.

In the fourteenth century, raiders drove out the rulers of Kanem, set up a new capital, and gave the kingdom a new name: Bornu. The invaders were forced out in the sixteenth century, and the kingdom was reestablished under the name Kanem-Bornu. The empire further expanded and was strong enough to fight off raids from militant Fulani nomads. When

This photo of modern-day Timbuktu shows that now, as in the fourteenth century, the city is a place to exchange goods and ideas.

Europeans arrived at Lake Chad, they had never heard of Kanem-Bornu, or its leader at the time, el-Kanemi. But, because his kingdom was so central to the trans-Saharan trade, and so many people passed through it, el-Kanemi had heard of the Europeans.

The Trade Routes

It's nearly impossible to describe the trans-Saharan trade routes in their entirety. The different caravans traveled along multiple routes, moving east, west, north, and south. All these routes had the same goals, to move goods and people from the coast inland, and inland out to the coast. The important stopping points along these routes changed over time, as the politics and economics of the region changed. That said, there were consistent patterns that all the different routes followed. The trade routes went from the major cities along the coast to trade centers in the Northern Sahara, then from these trade centers across the main part of the Sahara to trade centers in the Sudan, in the southern part of the desert. Finally, they went from these trade centers to export centers farther south. Along the way, there were oases and highlands that offered places to rest and goods of their own to trade, like dates and salt.

The most important places along the Mediterranean coast were capitals like Cairo in Egypt and Marrakesh and Fez in Morocco. Egypt, Libya, and Morocco received the majority of caravan traffic traveling to the coast. Farther away from the coast, into the desert, oasis towns like Sijilmasa and Wargla helped to connect and develop the trans-Saharan trade route. These towns remained important for a while as the trade routes expanded. Other vital stops along the way were Wadan, Gao, and Timbuktu.

Chapter 3

Salt, Slaves, Gold

Mediterranean merchants gave buyers in the southern Sahara cloth, glassware, ceramics, horses, as well as other goods useful for daily life. In exchange, the merchants got valuable commodities such as gold and slaves. (Slaves were often traded from areas that didn't have any gold to trade.) Between 800 and 1500 CE, approximately one ton of gold per year was carried across the Sahara due to the great demand for gold in Europe. Europeans also traded gold from Africa to India and China for spices and textiles. Therefore, the trans-Saharan trade routes played an important role in not only the local, but also the global economy.

Other commodities traded across the Sahara were goatskins, ivory, and ostrich feathers. These were valuable and played an important part in the economy of the slave trade. Yet they weren't

Opposite: *Work in the salt mines has changed little over the centuries.*

nearly as important as the salt, gold, and slaves that dominated the trade routes for so many centuries.

Salt

One of the roads leading out of Timbuktu heads north, through the oasis town of Arawan, to the salt mines of Taoudenni. The road is often covered with sand, making it much the same as it was during the peak of the trans-Saharan trade route. From Timbuktu, a camel caravan, then and now, would have to travel for at least a week before it got to Arawan. Once they arrived, they would likely stay there for at least a week, maybe more, to rest and recover. The next oasis was 800 miles (1,287.5 km) farther north.

What would make the difficult journey across the Sahara worthwhile? Salt. During the era of the trans-Saharan trade routes, salt would have been a critical part of people's diets. Salt also used to be very important for preserving food. Before refrigerators were invented, people had two main ways of storing food: pack it in ice, or dry it with salt. There was, of course, no ice in the desert. People had to use salt.

From Arawan, a caravan would continue north to the salt mines of Taoudenni. That mine is still operating today, in much the same way it operated hundreds of years ago. Merchants would load slabs of salt on the back of camels and either return to Timbuktu or continue even farther north, to Arab cities still thirty days away.

Salt was also coveted by the people of the grasslands and the forests south of the desert. Salt was in short supply in that region, making it very desired and therefore very valuable. The people south of the desert might not have had salt, but they had something that the merchants of Timbuktu wanted. In fact, merchants all over the world wanted what they had: gold. Since salt is necessary for human life, and people in the Sahel didn't have any, they were willing to pay a high price to get it. They were willing to pay in gold. In fact, for much of the history of the trade routes, salt and gold were worth the same. A slab of salt was equal to a bar of gold.

Gold

You can't eat gold, of course, and you don't need gold to live. However, people like gold, and they have from the beginning of recorded history. The rulers of West Africa knew the gold was important and did their best to keep the sources of the gold hidden from outsiders. They told many stories and legends about where the gold came from. Stories like the claim that there was a gold plant that blossomed after it rained and had "leaves like grass and roots of gold." Another legend said that the gold was carried from the mines by bird feathers. In reality, West African gold came from the Niger, Senegal, and Volta Rivers. And it wasn't even that hard to get to in many places because much of it was just below the surface.

In places where the gold was spread out, near the surface, the gold was panned from rivers like the Niger and the Senegal, or shallow excavations not more than 40 feet (12.2 m) deep. Miners worked in tunnels half filled with water. They would dig the ore with short handled pick axes and float the ore in baskets. The baskets were pulled to the surface by women, who washed it and guarded it until merchants came to

3 Grand pectoral en or
Musée de l'Institut Français
d'Afrique Noire, Dakar

Gold jewelry from the fifteenth century

collect it. There were larger deposits of gold near the
Volta, deposits deep enough that teams of workers
were needed to mine the ore. Some of these workers
were slaves, another valuable commodity on the
trade routes.

Gold built the ancient kingdoms of Old Ghana and Mali. Later it was gold that passed through Timbuktu and helped it grow into an important center of culture and learning. Timbuktu gained such a reputation for its wealth that travelers described the houses there as covered with gold. Though this was an exaggeration, it demonstrated the reputation that Timbuktu had built for itself. From Timbuktu, gold was carried north to Mediterranean ports, and from there to Spain, Italy, France, and other parts of Europe.

Gold from West Africa was not only important to local kingdoms and merchants, it was vital to the economies of the Mediterranean, the Middle East, and even Asia. Much of the currency of the Mediterranean and Europe was made from gold. India and China even traded for West African gold. The trade routes that carried gold across the Sahara were essential to the world's economy, as important then as Wall Street is to us today. During the Middle Ages, when the trade route was at its most important, two-thirds of the world's gold came from West Africa.

Slaves

Along with salt and gold, slaves were an important part of the economy of the trans-Saharan trade routes. Slavery is a tragic fact of human history: almost all human societies at one time or another had slaves. That doesn't make it right, of course, rather it reminds us that it is not a problem isolated to any one time or place.

Even though there were slaves from the beginnings of human history, not all slavery looked the same. In

North Africa, there were slaves before the beginning of the trans-Saharan slave trade. Yet it was Arab traders that really established a market for slaves.

Almost all societies used slaves, but not all people were subjected to slavery. For example, in Muslim societies, Muslims and other "People of the Book," like Jews and Christians, were not allowed to be used as slaves. Therefore, as Arab Muslims took over parts of North Africa and won converts (at times through force), the supply of slaves had to come from somewhere else.

Arab slave traders bought slaves from chiefs of weaker, less organized societies. Many slaves passed through Timbuktu. Like salt and gold, the slave trade helped merchants in cities like Timbuktu become rich. Merchant families operated slave pens on the edge of the city. For some of these merchants, buying and selling slaves was the main way they made money. They would buy slaves at a market and move them to wherever there was a demand. Some of the wealthy people in Timbuktu traded horses—a sign of wealth and prestige—for slaves.

Slavery remained a major part of the economy of North Africa up until 1900. There was strong demand in parts of the Middle East, Europe, and kingdoms across the region. The majority of slaves carried across the desert were female, destined to work in the houses of the wealthy. Those who worked as laborers worked in gardens, in salt mines, as part of caravan crews, and in gold mines. Later, they worked in cotton fields. Some men were forced to serve in the military, fighting for rulers as far away as Iraq.

Even though slaves in North Africa were often given the chance to gain their freedom, and even though some formers slaves went on to become successful merchants themselves, the slave trade was still very unjust and harsh. Slaves forced from West Africa to the Middle East or Mediterranean died from exposure to the different climate and unfamiliar diseases in their new surroundings. Many also died due to the rigors of the journey itself.

The Link Between Horses and Slavery

The horse played a major role in the slave trade. They were not only traded in Timbuktu, but all throughout the desert. Horses were also used to carry out raids and capture slaves. Although many goods like salt, gold, swords, and armor were exchanged for slaves, it was the horse that was traded most often. Anywhere from ten to thirty slaves were traded for one horse.

The majority of slaves exchanged in the slave trade came from areas just east of the Niger River—just east of Timbuktu. This wasn't because rulers in those areas were more cruel, or rulers in other areas were less cruel. It was because the areas east of the river didn't have any gold. Therefore, rulers didn't have anything to trade other than slaves.

The Business of the Caravans

The Sahara is often compared to the sea, and camels were given the nickname "ships of the desert." Camels were owned by nomads. The merchants who conducted the slave trade did not buy camels from the Bedouins, rather they rented them, along with the services of the nomads who owned them.

The caravans that carried the goods were not owned or controlled by any one group. Instead, they

Camels are still often used for transportation in the desert.

were composed of several merchants working together. Caravans were made up of one thousand to five thousand camels and several hundred people. If at all possible, they would try to travel in the winter, when the weather was cooler. Even then, they would rest in the afternoon to avoid traveling in the hottest part of

the day. A caravan would travel about 15 to 25 miles (24 to 40 km) per day. At that pace, it would take around seventy days to travel from the northern to the southern part of the Sahara. That means that a place like Timbuktu might see no more than one or two caravans per year. Yet even one visit from a caravan with five thousand camels would have a big impact.

The caravans helped to build the wealth of cities at both ends of the trade routes, as well as strategically located cities like Timbuktu in between. The caravans also helped to spread Islam from the Middle East across the region, and with it the Arabic language.

In the early days of Saharan trade, business was more informal. There were no set prices, everything was negotiated and no written records were kept. In order to get access to an area, a merchant or trader needed to know someone personally. They might also have to pay a very high fee for the privilege of doing business in a certain place.

As Islam and the Arabic language spread, different tribes were united under a common identity. Before that time, two people might not trust each other because they came from a different tribe and spoke a different language. Now they could meet with the shared understanding that they were both Muslim. As the culture become relatively more similar, so too did the business practices. Uniform prices could be set, rather than changing from place to place and person to person. This made trade more predictable and transparent. Islam also made the region more peaceful and, therefore, more stable. There were Berbers who resisted Islam and others who followed different versions of Islam. However, Islam largely brought people together (after the initial conquest, at least). Skirmishes gave way to increased cooperation in the name of increased trade.

Imports

As salt, gold, and slaves left Africa, textiles came in. Fabrics from the Europe were in great demand. In fact, there was such a great demand that local cities, like Timbuktu, began to produce their own fabrics. Cotton could be grown locally, and the skills needed to produce the fabrics could be learned quickly. However, there was not a wide variety of colors to choose from. The only local source of dye was the indigo plant, and the deep blue color that this plant produced suited local tastes. The Tuareg nomads came to be identified by their dark blue clothing.

Another important import from Europe was the cowrie shell. **Cowrie shells** were small shells harvested from near the Maldives Islands near India. These shells came across the desert in caravans, then later, in greater numbers, by ship. Upon arrival, they were used as currency.

Other kinds of currency were used at the time. Imported coins, strips of cloth, and iron bars were all circulated. Cowries were desirable because they were cheaper, lighter, more durable, and difficult to copy. As the economy shifted from an informal and relational system to one that was more uniform and widespread, a common currency became very important.

Chapter 4

The Major Players

Trade routes like those that spanned the Sahara involved several towering figures in the early history of the region. Rulers including Mansa Musa, Ali Beeri, and Mulay Ahmad al-Mansur played a role in shaping the trade routes, as did empires like the Mali and the Songhai. This chapter takes a closer look at the people involved in the trans-Saharan trade routes and the geographic locations central to trade.

Mansa Musa

Mansa Musa was one of the greatest rulers of the West African kingdom of Mali. He ruled from 1312 to 1337, and the time of his rule is considered to be the golden age of Mali. Mansa Musa was young, handsome, and very wealthy. He lived in a

Opposite: *A Tuareg man walks the alleys of Timbuktu.*

magnificent palace, ruled over a large territory, and had twenty-four kings serving under him.

When he went out among the people, he rode on horseback and carried gold weapons. Those included a bow and arrows, which were more likely symbols of royal power rather than tools that were actually useful for hunting. When he was in his palace, he sat on an ebony throne on a platform with elephant tusks on the side. There were dozens of slaves behind him, from as far away as Turkey and Egypt. One of the slaves had the job of holding a large sunshade over the *mansa's* head.

The lower kings sat in two rows on either side, and next to them were military commanders. In front of the king was an executioner carrying a sword, as well as a spokesman called a *jeli*. It was the jeli's job to repeat what the mansa said because the mansa did not speak out loud in public. Instead, he would whisper in the jeli's ear, and the jeli would announce what he had said.

Music followed the mansa wherever he went. Drums, trumpets made from elephant tusks, and a xylophone-type instrument called a *bala* provided the soundtrack to life in the palace. There were also always two horses tied nearby. At the time, horses were very valuable and prestigious. Even though the mansa would only ever be able to ride one horse at a time, he traveled with two as yet another way to display his fabulous wealth.

Mansa Musa's Pilgrimage

Mansa Musa was a very devout Muslim. He made the pilgrimage to Mecca, as all Muslims are expected to do at least once in their lifetime. Mansa Musa set out on his pilgrimage in 1323; it would take him over one year to complete his journey with an elaborate caravan. He traveled with thousands of people, including one of his wives, Inari Kanute, who brought hundreds of slaves with her. In addition, there were many other Muslims from the royal court, along with merchants, soldiers, servants, and other slaves.

The caravan also had thousands of animals like camels and donkeys that carried food, water, and at least eighty loads of gold dust. Yet that was not the only gold. Mansa Musa brought a tremendous amount of gold in different forms along on the trek. He gave the sultan of Egypt forty thousand gold coins as a gift, and he gave ten thousand gold coins to the sultan's deputy. His entourage spent so much other gold in the local markets that the value of gold declined because there was suddenly so much of it. It did not regain its value for several years.

Mansa Musa was so proud and so powerful that he refused to follow the custom of kissing the ground in front of the Egyptian sultan when visiting. He said he would only bow down to the God who created him. He eventually met with the sultan and bowed down, but only to pray. The sultan was impressed with Mansa Musa's wealth and devotion and presented him with many expensive gifts in return.

Though Mansa Musa was one of the most powerful people to make the long journey across the Sahara, even he and his caravan were not able to do so without hardship. All told, on his pilgrimage (which went beyond the Sahara and into the Arabian Peninsula), Mansa Musa lost one-third of his people and animals, and he spent all of his gold.

In spite of this, he did not return home empty handed. He brought back four descendants of

The annual pilgrimage to Mecca attracts millions of devout Muslims each year.

Muhammed after he offered to pay their way. He also returned with an architect named Abu Ishaq al-Sahili. Al-Sahili built Mansa Musa a new house in Timbuktu. Rectangular with a dome on top, covered in plaster and decorated with colorful designs, the style was copied by others and is still popular in the region.

Timbuktu and the Mali Empire

Timbuktu was a major stop on the trans-Saharan trade routes. Several different routes passed through the city, connecting people from many different parts of the desert. Nowadays, Timbuktu is perhaps best known as a faraway place, as in the expression "from here to Timbuktu." Today, it is far away from other large cities and it is difficult to get to, with only one paved road from the city, leading out to the airport.

In its heyday, though, Timbuktu was a major center of trans-Saharan trade and Islamic learning. Caravans of thousands of camels would ride into town, bringing with them a city's worth of visitors. Merchants in Timbuktu built great warehouses to hold goods for trading, as well as space for camels. Upstairs there were apartments for the merchants and their servants. Some larger merchant associations had similar warehouses at many points along the caravan routes. The population of Timbuktu would grow by fifteen thousand people when the caravans were in town.

The route from Morocco to Timbuktu took close to two months. That means the merchants and camel drivers who made their living on these routes would spend four to six months at a time away from their homes and families. Mansa Musa could afford to travel with an entourage, but most people could not. Life on the caravan could be lonely and dangerous.

Since the trip was perilous and took such an effort, merchants would have to wait until they assembled a large enough caravan to make the trip worth their while. Sometimes this would take months, and at times such delays would occur in the middle of the trip.

Leo Africanus

Leo Africanus was a former slave and papal scribe. He was born al-Hasan ibn Muhammed al-Wazzan az-Zayyati in 1485 in Granada, Spain. He went to school in Morocco and traveled throughout the Sahara with his uncle, making it as far south as Mali. When he was captured by pirates, Africanus was sold to the pope as a slave. The pope freed him, and Africanus wrote a book about his travels. Titled *History and Description of Africa and the Curious Things Therein*

Leo Africanus wrote some of earliest outsider accounts of life in the Sahara.

Contained, it was, at the time, the only eyewitness account of the continent available to Europeans. Africanus told of the great cities of the Sahel, including the thriving commercial center of Timbuktu:

> The royal court is magnificent and very well organized. When the king goes from one city to another with the people of his court, he rides a camel and the horses are led by hand by servants. If fighting becomes necessary, the servants mount the camels and all the soldiers mount on horseback. When someone wishes to speak to the king, he must kneel before him and bow down; but this is only required of those who have never before spoken to the king, or of ambassadors. The king has about 3,000 horsemen and infinity of foot-soldiers armed with bows ... which they use to shoot poisoned arrows. This king makes war only upon neighboring enemies and upon those who do not want to pay him tribute. When he has gained a victory, he has all of them—even the children—sold in the market at Timbuktu.

Merchants would have to stay in strange cities like Timbuktu, eating, sleeping, buying and selling, and otherwise contributing to the life and economy of their temporary home.

At the peak of its power, the empire of Mali covered a large part of the southern Sahara—"Its length being four month's journey and its width likewise," according to one account. However, Mali declined for the same reason so many great powers have declined throughout history: it was too large. Its territory was too vast, and it became impossible to govern the outermost provinces, which ended up breaking away.

The Songhai Empire

The Songhai Empire filled the void left by Mali. The Songhai was originally settled by three different ethnic groups that arrived in the area at different times. The Sorko settled on the banks of the Niger River and spent much of their time in canoes on the water. They were experts at fishing and navigating the river. The Gow came next. They were skilled hunters, and they thrived by killing river animals like crocodiles and hippopotamuses. The third group in the area was the Do (Doh). Their specialty was farming, and the flood plains of the Niger were a great place to raise crops.

In the tenth century, a fourth group, the Songhai, moved into the area. They were more powerful, and thanks in part to their skill at riding horses, they were able to take control of the area and the three other groups. Soon, all the people spoke the same language and called themselves Songhai.

Ali Beeri

After Mali withdrew, local leaders known as *sii* took power. One of the most powerful was Ali Beeri (Ali "the Great"), an ambitious military leader who commanded troops on boats and on horseback. Once Sii Ali consolidated his power in Goa, he looked to take control of other important trading centers in the region, including Timbuktu.

The Tuareg were in control of Timbuktu in the time before the Songhai empire. The wealthiest citizens of the city, Muslim merchants, scholars, and religious officials, worked with the Tuareg to resist Sii Ali and his army. When he invaded, they fled into the desert to the city of Walata, another important commercial center. By 1469, Sii Ali was in control of Timbuktu, and the Songhai were well on their way to having an empire.

The next commercial center Sii Ali targeted was Djenné. Djenné was built on the floodplain between the Niger and Bani rivers. The city was surround by a high wall. During the wet season when the rivers flooded, it was surrounded by water. Sii Ali used the flooding to his advantage, however, moving on the city with boats. The attackers were unable to get past the city wall, but they were able to seal off the city and prevent goods, people, and food from coming or going. After four years, the people of Djenné, weak from hunger, surrendered.

From the city of Djenné, Sii Ali moved on to Walata. He wanted to attack by boat, even though there were no natural waterways leading to Walata. Thus, he ordered his men to build canals. While they were building the canal, he got word that a rival kingdom was planning to attack. He left the canal project to go fight that battle. He defeated his rival but never returned to finish the canal.

In spite of this, Sii Ali conquered a vast territory, and with that came the problem of ruling such a large swath of land. Ali spent most of his time traveling and fighting battles against local uprisings of the hostile neighbors who resented the Songhai presence in their territory. He died while returning home from one such battle.

Sii Ali's son took power, but he was soon replaced by an army commander named Muhammad Toure. Toure took the title *askia*. Though "askia" was originally a military title, from that time forward, it became the title by which all Songhai rulers were known.

Askia Muhammad

Askia Muhammad continued to expand the Songhai Empire. He was known as Muhammed the Great, and he expanded well beyond the territory established by Sii Ali. Along with focusing on expansion, he built a professional army to defend the empire. Askia Muhammad funded his operations by collecting tributes from the kings he brought under his control. The empire grew so large that it was divided into an eastern half with a capital in Goa, and a western half with a capital in Timbuktu.

Askia Muhammed had thirty-seven sons with his many wives and concubines. The sons had eyes on his throne, and many pressured him to retire and fought amongst themselves about who would take over. Muhammed grew physically weak and by the time he was seventy years old, he went blind. Unable to hold on to power himself, and with the support of his people slipping, Muhammad had little choice but to give up control. He passed his power on to his oldest son, Musa. Musa began killing many of his half-brothers, and he was eventually killed in battle, less than three years after he took power. He was replaced by a cousin who was overthrown by another one of Muhammed's sons, Ismail. Ismail also reigned for less than three years, though he died a natural death.

Another son, Ishaq, took over. He ruled with a heavy hand, inspiring fear and creating many enemies. He regularly sent agents to Timbuktu to extort large sums of money from merchants, even though Islam has strict prohibitions against such a practice. In addition to angering the merchants of Timbuktu, the amount of money Ishaq forcefully collected was a burden on the economy of the city and the empire as a whole. He controlled the opposition by exiling or killing anyone who defied him. When he died, another brother, Daud, took his place.

Daud was the last son of Muhammed the Great to be askia of Songhai. One of his sons followed him, and his descendants ruled until the end of the kingdom in 1591.

The Moroccan Invasion of Songhai

According to seventeenth-century historians, sometime in 1589 a slave from Songhai escaped captivity in the desert and fled to Morocco. This slave, Wuld Kirinfil, wrote a letter to the sultan of Morocco, Mulay Ahmad al-Mansur. The letter encouraged the sultan to invade Songhai. The sultan wrote to the ruler of Songhai at the time, Askia Ishaq II, demanding he pay a tax on

The architecture of Timbuktu preserves some of the history of mighty West African empires.

every camel-load of salt that came out of the disputed salt mine of Taghaza.

The askia responded by sending a spear and a pair of iron sandals and the message that he would pay the tax as soon as the sultan wore through the sandals. Since the sandals were iron, this was a creative way

of saying no to the sultan's demands. The sultan had heard stories about Songhai's wealth, particularly the gold. The askia's defiance gave al-Mansur the reason he needed to invade.

The sultan of Morocco attacked with an army of four thousand men, including two thousand soldiers armed with muskets and five hundred men on horseback. It took ten thousand camels to carry all the army's supplies. They carried tents, food, and water enough to last them the forty-day journey across the desert. They also brought gunpowder and four small cannons, weapons imported to Morocco from Spain. There had never been weapons like that in the Southern Sahara. The Songhai were overwhelmed by the noise alone.

The Moroccan army won a decisive victory on March 12, 1591, near the town of Tondibi, 30 miles (48.3 km) north of Goa. The Songhai army fought bravely against the overwhelming strength of the Moroccans, but they were forced to retreat across the Niger River. Askia Ishaq made one final attempt to appease the Moroccans. He offered Jawar Pasha, the commander of their army, 100,000 gold pieces and 1,000 slaves in the hopes that they would be satisfied and return to Morocco. The Moroccan army was exhausted following their trip across the desert and the battles that followed. Jawar Pasha was ready to accept the offer, but the sultan wanted to keep control of the newly conquered territory.

When Sultan al-Mansur rejected the offer, he replaced Jawar Pasha with Mahmud Pasha and gave the new commander instructions to finish the invasion. The Moroccan army invaded and looted Goa, Djenné, and Timbuktu. They brought the riches taken from these cities back to Marrakesh, the capital of Morocco, where the sultan used it to build several palaces.

The Songhai army did not give up control of their empire without a fight. They fled into the countryside and continued to resist the Moroccan invasion. They also rebelled against Askia Ishaq, who they felt was a weak leader. They replaced him with Muhammed Gao. Muhammed Gao was invited to meet with

Mahmud Pasha, but it was a trap. Muhammed Gao was assassinated.

Gao's brother, Askia Nuh, took over. The Songhai continued their resistance for years, fighting battles in the desert and stopping the Moroccans from taking control of more territory. However, the Songhai were never able to regain control. Timbuktu and other urban trading centers remained in the hands of the Moroccans, and the rest of the Songhai empire broke apart into smaller states. By the eighteenth century, there was nothing left of the Songhai Empire.

Chapter 5

The Effects of the Trans-Saharan Trade Routes

The largest and most lasting effect of the trans-Saharan trade routes was the spread of Islam across North Africa. By the end of the trade routes' peak, Islam had spread all the way to the Atlantic coast, into Spain, and down to present day Sudan.

The Varieties of Islam

Islam, and with it the Arabic language, acted as a unifying force across the region in many respects. Yet from its beginning, the religion has been divided into different interpretations and sects. All the different sects made their way to Africa. In fact,

Opposite: *Daily prayer is a cornerstone of a devout Muslim's life.*

The Foundations of Islam

Islam is, generally speaking, a religion "of the book." This means it is a religion in which teachings are written down in a collection of sacred writings, much like Judaism and Christianity. While Jewish people have the Torah, and Christians have the Bible, Muslims have the **Koran**. Muslims consider the Koran to be the written word of God (or *Allah*, which is simply Arabic for God), dictated to the Prophet Muhammad and written down by his hand. Muslims believe the Koran to be the highest and fullest revelation of God, and Muhammad to be "the seal of the Prophets." No further revelation can be as complete, and no translation can be as complete as the original Koran, which was written in Arabic. For that reason, the spread of Islam meant the spread of Arabic. Even Muslims who never used Arabic in their day-to-day lives would learn at least some Arabic to recite prayers or read the Koran.

The holy life of an individual Muslim is built around what is known as the Five Pillars. The first is Shahadah, reciting the Muslim statement of faith ("There is no god but Allah and Muhammad is the messenger of Allah"). Salat is the performance of ritual prayers five times per day. Zakat involves giving alms (or paying a tax) to help the poor. Sawm is fasting during the holy month of Ramadan. And the fifth pillar is **hajj**, making a pilgrimage to the holy city of Mecca at least once in one's lifetime. The fifth pillar is especially important to the history of the trade routes, as it gave Muslims a religious obligation to travel across the desert.

some scholars refer to the spread of Muslims rather than the spread of Islam because there was never only one form of Islam.

The majority of Muslims are **Sunni**. They follow the teachings and traditions of the caliphs who succeeded Muhammad. The major dissenting branch is **Shia**. Shia Muslims follow a different line of succession. They believe that Ali, Muhammed's son-in-law, was his rightful successor. The division between Sunni and Shia has led to political conflicts and different interpretations of Islamic teaching and law. A third group, and one that had much support in North Africa, is the Kharaj. The Kharijites refused to submit to either of the traditional authorities.

Transfers of Power

Soon after Muslims took control of North Africa, they faced rebellion from local Berbers. Many Berbers were drawn to the Muslim faith but put off by foreign rule. Therefore, they gravitated toward the Kharaj. The Kharijites soon became a force in the countryside. They even controlled important commercial centers near the coast for a while. The moderate Ibadi sect gained influence among the Kharaj and eventually formed an independent state, Tahert. From this base of power, the Ibadi were able to push into the desert. They traded with non-Muslim tribes, shared Islam, and won converts.

Meanwhile, in Morocco, in the eighth century, a group called the Idrissids claimed to be descended from Ali. They were the first North Africa rulers to follow the Shia faith. Though they did not establish a far-reaching or long-lasting empire, they did extend the reach of Islam farther west than it had ever been.

The Almohades regime also advanced a of version of Shiism. The founder of the Almohades, Ibn Toumert, drew on several different Shia teachings. He did not, however, claim to be descended from Ali. Rather, he followed and earlier breakaway sect called the Fatimid Caliphate. This group claimed to follow Ismail, a later imam (religious leader) descended from Ali. The Almohades were successful in uniting most of the northern Maghreb and southern Spain. They were not able to maintain power, though. Soon stricter, more orthodox teachings took over.

In 1050, a tribal confederation known as the Banu Hilal invaded North Africa. Starting in Egypt and moving across the desert westward, the Banu Hilal looted and pillaged almost every town and city in its path. Tribes in the path of this invasion were faced with choice to either convert and assimilate or to flee. Some tribes like the Nmadi ended up as servants. Others, like the Dogon in the far south of the Sahara, moved high up on cliffs to escape the invaders. To this day, the Dogon live on the cliffs, high and far away from other civilizations. Some Berbers retreated farther into the desert, followed by these more orthodox Muslims who were more interested in converting "pagans" than trading with them. Every part of the desert was influenced by Arabs eventually. Some groups like the Tuareg and Tubu held out longer than others or only adapted a version of Islam more suitable to them. Other groups claimed the Arab identity, even if they were not ethnically Arab. To be "Arab" was thought to be powerful, aristocratic, and superior.

Many people, kings included, converted to Islam while still following some of their traditional practices. Kings had the challenge of ruling a people who followed the traditional tribal religions, as well as engaging an outside world that was increasingly Muslim. Since North African kings kept no written records in the ninth, tenth, and eleventh centuries, it is impossible to know the degree to which they were truly devoted to Islam. The best indicators we have are the historical accounts of pilgrimages, such as the one Mansa Musa took in the 1320s.

Sufism

Another form of Islam that took hold in North Africa was **Sufism**. *Suf* means wool, a rough fabric worn by ascetics, people who renounce worldly comfort. Sufis believe that by withdrawing from the **secular** world one could become closer to God. At first, Sufis were considered heretics and their writings were burned. But their teachings eventually found a following, and schools of Sufi thought sprang up across the region.

Some Sufi teachings were useful in blending Islam with traditional religions. This practice of blending ideas from one religion with ideas from a new religion is known as **syncretism**. Sufis practiced *dhikr* and saint worship. Dhikr consists of chanting certain religious phrases while dancing. The goal of dhikr is to reach an altered state of mind and in that way grow closer to God. Dhikr would have looked and sounded familiar to people who also used music, chanting, and dance in their traditional religious ceremonies.

Sufis also built tombs for *walis*, or saints. Some tombs were said to contain the remains of leaders like Uqba ibn Nafi, one of the early Arab leaders, or Idris I of Morocco. Others were said to be for religious leaders who were thought to be especially holy. Building shrines to the dead was also a traditional religious practice. By building tombs for walis, Sufis were blending the beliefs of the old and new systems.

As with most religions, the teachings of Islam can be taken literally or more symbolically. In Islam, these are recognized as **zahir** (visible) and **batin** (concealed) meanings. There were the written words of the Koran, for example, and the lessons they taught. Then there was the batin meaning, which could be found by binding Koranic verses in leather amulets, or decoding them with secret patter, or washing them in special potions. Such practices were very similar to traditional practices. By using both zahir and batin meaning, people could embrace the new religion of Islam while still maintaining some of their traditional practices and beliefs.

Islamicate Culture

Scholars have a word for cultures that are heavily influenced by Islam, but not completely defined by it: **Islamicate**. Islamicate cultures have different religions, different ethnic groups, different languages, and different political systems that had been established well before the arrival of Islam. They have maintained their traditional identity to varying degrees (some became more Muslim, some remained more traditional). Yet they are Islamicate because they have all been in constant contact with Islam and Arabic culture.

Before the Arabs invaded, much of North Africa was Christian, with many traditional religions and a large Jewish presence also found there. There were not many Christians left after the Arab invasion. Traditional religions became more isolated or survived

Mosques come in different shapes and sizes, but all provide a space for study and prayer.

by adopting some parts of Islam. Only Judaism was able to maintain its adherents, though they were not a large part of the population.

Only about 2 percent of the population of North Africa was Jewish, but this was enough to have an impact on the trade routes. Some of the wealthier members of the Jewish community were merchants who established a trade network across the region. However, the majority of Jewish people were craftsman who made metal or leather goods. Jewish merchants were primarily active as importers. Some Jewish merchants and tradesman would have traveled the length of the trade routes, no doubt, but there is no evidence of widespread Jewish travel. Among other reasons, devoted Jews would not have traveled on the Sabbath. This would have made an already long trip even longer. There are records of Jewish people being active in Timbuktu, but no established settlements, communities, or even congregations.

As Muslim merchants crossed the desert, many of the major commercial centers also became centers of Muslim learning. This was the case with Timbuktu. **Mosques** in Timbuktu and other urban areas were incubators of literacy, places where people read and produced books. Most of these books were religious in nature, but some were historical chronicles. Much of what historians know about this period comes from the histories and biographies written by scholars in and around mosques.

Language, Arts, and Architecture Along the Trade Routes

Arabs not only brought with them a culture of the written word, they also brought a culture of secular oral poetry. This poetry was especially popular among the nomadic Arabs. Muslim scholars began to put this poetry into writing. By the fifteenth century, these texts were popular among urban aristocrats and were read as entertainment at cafes or during special events such as weddings. These later audiences would not necessarily be familiar with background of the stories and characters celebrated in the poems. Thus, the performer would have to create an elaborate but easy-to-understand backstory. In this way, the tales grew from short poems to epics. These epics were especially popular among the Banu Hilal, who used them to recount the glory of their conquests across the desert.

Islam mixed with, influenced, and even dominated the other cultures along the trans-Saharan trade routes. But it did not erase them entirely. The most widespread language group prior to the arrival of the Arabs were Berbers. All Berber speakers were related linguistically, but it is probably more accurate to describe Berber as a family of languages. Pockets of Berbers were able to resist the influence of Islam in part because they were so numerous and so widespread. Even though Arabic became the most widespread and official language across the desert, local languages did not disappear entirely. The more isolated the group, the more their local language was preserved. The more contact a group had with the outside world, the more they spoke Arabic.

The Turaeg, who remained fiercely independent, maintained a writing system known as Tifinagh. This language was used mostly in the home, mostly by women. Outside of the home it was used informally, graffiti-style, written on rocks or in sand to communicate with travelers. The Tuareg also had an oral tradition in which the history of the people was passed down in the form of poems, stories, and songs. They were never written down, however.

Mande and Praise Poetry

Arabic was used all across the desert, but there were four main languages used to conduct business regionally. Mande was the first Sudanic language to be used in trans-Saharan trade transactions. Mande is further divided into the Bambara, Malinke, and Dyula dialects, and the more distinct Soninke language.

Griots are like walking books, telling the myths, legends, and stories of the people.

It was Soninke that was used in Old Ghana, and merchants from Old Ghana spoke Soninke when they made deals in the gold fields. When Mali replaced Ghana as the regional power, Malinke replaced Soninke as dominant language.

In Mande culture, certain talents such as blacksmithing, leatherwork, and being able to perform music, tell stories, or recite poetry were valued above other skills. Only particular groups were permitted to learn these skills. These groups were called **nyamakalaw**. Members of these groups were not allowed to marry outside of the group, and they were not to hold political office.

Other groups also had similar divisions. The Tuareg, Fulani, and Hassani also considered artisans to be set apart from the rest of society. These distinctions were in place long before the arrival of Islam. They allowed for cultures like the Mande to adapt quickly to the religion. For example, the Muslim **ulama**, or scholars, were seen as another type of nyamakalaw.

The Mande had (and have) a written language, but most of their literary achievements were oral. The storytellers that performed epics such as the epic of Sunjata, the Lion King, were nyamakalaw. Now known as **griots**, they were once known by the Mande term *jeli*. Music was a big part of the presentation of an epic. Two of the main instruments used in these performances made their way to the Western Sudan via the trade routes. The **kora** is a harp with twenty-one or more strings, and the **koni** is a lute that is played much like a guitar. There is a record of similar instruments being found in earlier times in Egypt and North Africa, so it is possible that they were introduced to the Western Sudan by trade. However, scholars are not certain about the instrument's transmission. The koni was later brought to North America via the transatlantic slave trade where it became the precursor to the banjo.

In modern day, most griots are pious Muslims, and some of them perform only Islamic texts. Today, like yesterday, most griots tell the family histories of powerful men. In exchange, the powerful men support the griots. This type of poetry is called panegyric, or praise poetry. It is one of the most well developed forms of oral literature in all of Africa. The fourteenth-century Arab travel writer Ibn Battuta described panegyric in this way: "This throne on which you are sitting was sat on by such-and-such a king and his good deeds were so-and-so; so you do good deeds that will be remembered after you."

One of the functions of epic poetry is to tell obscure stories from the past. One of the terms the Mande use to describe the purpose of epics is *maana*, which is the same word Arab speakers use to describe the teaching of difficult to understand Islamic writings. This common word is evidence of the cultural exchange that took place along the trade routes.

The Fulani and Cultural Exchange

The Fulani are a nomadic group with disputed origins. Based in the Sahel, the southern fringe of the Sahara, some think they originally came from North Africa. Others believe they came from West and sub-Saharan Africa. Though they have some facial features that resemble Berbers, their language is in the same family as Mande. The Fulani, like many nomadic tribes, remain independent. The Fulani were the first African tribe to spread Islam by *jihad*, or holy war. They spread Islam to much of West Africa. As they did so, they also established and strengthened trade routes. Cattle is at the center of the life of the Fulani, and the more cattle one has, the wealthier one is.

After they converted to Islam, they started using the Arabic alphabet, but they also maintained their pre-Islamic oral traditions. The Fulani became dedicated to learning and spreading their new faith. As part of this effort, they worked to translate Islamic texts to their own language. At first, this was only done orally.

Traditional Fulani poetry is about cattle and the environment. Here is one example, translated by Christiane Seydou and quoted by Ralph Austen in *Trans-Saharan Africa in World History*:

> Send my excuses!
>
> As for me, since the dry season arrived I have been camped in the Great
> Seno region
>
> Having no other thoughts than to water my herd on the trickles of
> spring water.

Such poems are usually recited without musical accompaniment. As the Fulani came into contact with other traditions, they, too, began to incorporate music into their performances. Some Fulani epics are about Muslim leaders, but most are secular. Many of them uphold the values of *pulakuu*, or pre-Islamic ideas about manhood. Numerous Muslim scholars at the time disapproved of traditional epics. They felt the pulakuu were proof that the Fulani were uncivilized before they converted to Islam. However, traditional Fulani culture and Islam continued to influence each other and merged into a new culture.

The Architecture of Mosques

Islam, like many religions, requires sacred places to worship. Therefore, Muslim leaders built mosques soon after arriving in a city. The mosques were built according to local architectural practices, which often had less to do with making a stylistic statement and more to do with making the best use of the materials available. For example, mosques in the southern Sahara were built in a pyramid shape and had wooden poles called *toron* sticking out of them. These mosques look different than mosques anywhere else in the world, but they serve the same purpose: to provide a place for prayer and the studying of holy text.

The mosques were built from *banco*, bricks of clay dried by the sun. Bricks dried by fire would have been stronger, and builders would have happily used them, but there was not enough wood in the desert to fire enough bricks to meet all of the building needs. Banco can't support much weight. Therefore, larger buildings must be built in a pyramid shape so that they do not collapse. The bricks and clay get worn away during the rainy season. The toron are used to climb up to the top to make any needed repairs.

Though wood was used to fire bricks for special occasions, most wood was used for either iron smelting or carving. Iron was produced mainly for weapons and armor, though some was used for artistic purposes. The iron was either made into metal goods or made into tools used to carve wood.

An example of a banco structure

Woodcarving was a prominent art form in Central and West Africa in the fourteenth and fifteenth centuries.

Woodcarving is one of the best known artistic practices of Central and West Africa, but it is officially forbidden by some interpretations of Islam. Carvings of animals that were considered unclean, such as pigs, are forbidden because carving them was thought to be the same as eating them. Carvings of people were forbidden, because it was thought to be too close to the work of God, and only God can create people.

That said, African carving traditions influenced Islam in several ways. Some mosques had designs that looked like the horns of wild animals and leather workers decorated harnesses, armor, and book covers. Many of these decorations were abstract shapes inspired by woodcarvings but were different enough to be acceptable to orthodox Muslims.

At the same time, traditional artists were influenced by Islam. Hunters decorated their tunics with Islamic symbols alongside their own traditional symbols. Woodcarvers crafted figures of Muslim scholars to go with their traditional carvings of animals and spirits. Masks had verses from the Koran written on them.

The trade routes facilitated this dynamic cultural exchange across the Sahara. These exchanges were especially common in urban areas, like Timbuktu, where traditional cultures and Islamic cultures intermingled. This exchange continues to the present day, even though the economy of the Sahara and trade routes are very different now. The change that brought an end to the central role of the trans-Saharan trade route was the beginning of European colonization.

Chapter 6

The End of the Trans-Saharan Trade Routes

The beginning of the twentieth century marked the end of the trans-Saharan trade route. In 1823, a British explorer named Hugh Clapperton made his way across the Sahara and into present day Nigeria. He told the local sultan, Muhammed Bello, that he had come for reasons of science, to establish trade routes from the Sudan to the Atlantic Ocean, and to abolish the slave trade. Muslim traders warned the sultan that the British had come to take the country and disrupt the established trade routes. Sadly, they were right.

Opposite: *In World War I and World War II, battles were fought throughout North Africa. Here, a soldier stands guard during World War I.*

The Beginnings of the Colonial Era

The British had already taken over India and had been launching naval attacks against parts of North Africa. In 1827, another incident, this one involving the French in Algiers, sparked another wave of colonization. On April 29, 1827, the ruler of Algiers got into an argument with the French consul about debts. The ruler hit the consul with a fly swatter and threw him out. Three years later, the French sent troops to occupy Algeria. The French occupation lasted for decades and spread from Algeria to Tunisia and Morocco and south into the Sahara.

Far more serious was the Berlin Congo Conference that took place between November 15, 1884, and February 26, 1885. The conference was given the nickname the "Scramble for Africa." Fifteen European countries along with the United States met to negotiate how they would divide up the region. Europe and North America had just gone through the industrial revolution. Both continents had an interest in finding new markets overseas, as well as the technology to be able to do it. The internal politics of Europe were also a driving force behind **colonialism**.

Take that dispute with the fly swatter, for example. The argument was about payment for a shipment of grain from North Africa to the French army in the 1790s. France pressed the issue in 1827 and went to war in 1830, not because they needed the money, but because King Charles X wanted to give his regime a boost in popularity. The plan didn't work, though, and the regime fell in 1830.

Colonialism and War

France was a prominent leader among the nations scrambling for Africa. European nations felt internal threats from socialist rebellions. As a response to this perceived threat, they sought new markets overseas and new sources of raw materials. There were also rivalries among the nations, particularly between the countries of Western Europe and Germany. This was due to the fact that Germany was emerging as a major new economic power. One of the goals of the Berlin Congo Conference was to give every European nation

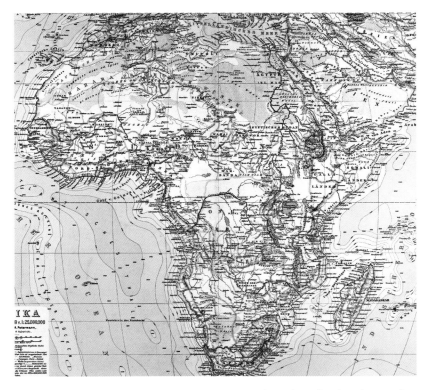

In the early twentieth century, European colonialism had redrawn the map of most of Africa.

a part of Africa. In doing so, every European nation would get a piece of the prosperity from the new African colonies. This plan did not work, and World War I started in 1914. Countries allied with France fought with countries allied with Germany. Some of that fighting took place in North Africa.

Although they were allies during the war, France and England were economic rivals before and after the war. They each tried to use their African colonies to best the other. France, which gained the most territory in the scramble for Africa, had grand plans to build a trans-Saharan railroad. This railroad was supposed to connect Timbuktu with Algiers and give France easy access to the people and resources of the Sudan. It was also supposed to give France a political and economic advantage over the British and help them subdue the Tuareg, ever resistant to outside control over their lives.

The Disruption of the Trade Routes

Europeans had been actively exploring the Sahara since the eighteenth century. One of the biggest reasons behind European exploration was the search for a route on which to build a trans-Saharan railroad. Some Europeans, like Clapperton, were successful. However, many were killed by Tuareg nomads. In 1880, Colonel Paul Flatter and his men were attacked while looking for a route through the desert. The survivors were stranded and stayed alive by eating their dead companions.

Tracks were laid by the French from the Mediterranean coast into the northern Sahara, and by the British from the Atlantic into Nigeria. Yet neither

European countries, especially France, tried unsuccessfully to build a trans-Saharan railroad.

project came close to connecting the different sides of the desert. Still these rail projects, along with roads, were disruptive to trans-Saharan trade. Also disruptive to the traditional trade routes was the abolition of slavery, first in Europe, and then in the Ottoman Empire and Egypt.

The New Economic and Political Order

The disruption did not necessarily mean immediate economic hardship. Sudanic countries, instead of trading by camel north through the Maghreb, now traded by rail south to the Atlantic Ocean. Trains are much more efficient than camels, so countries in the Sudan could now trade more commodities. These included cotton and peanuts, in addition to traditional items, like goatskins.

Even caravan drivers benefitted initially. Colonial administrators used camel caravans to travel to hard to reach areas. And trade within the desert increased, with dates, salt, livestock, and handicrafts still being bought and sold locally.

While colonial rule brought some immediate, short-term benefits, it was not sustainable. The French, in order to increase cattle production, drilled new wells, and made existing wells deeper. The water was able to produce larger herds, but at the expense of overgrazing. This depleted the soil and grass, as well as the water supply. In the 1960s, there was another dry period. The drought resulted in an ecological disaster from which the region has still not recovered.

European nations did not necessarily benefit from colonial rule over trans-Saharan Africa, but private companies did. In Algeria, white settlers took over some of the best land. Even though they were not all French citizens, France gave these settlers privileges and protections as if they were. The wheat and wine that they produced competed with French wheat and wine. The white settlers were also given the political rights of French citizens, unlike the local Arab-Berber population.

There was little to no settlement in the interior of the desert, which meant these communities were able to better maintain their traditional way of life. But it also meant that they were cut off from any new economic development, most of which took place in the most populous areas on the edge of the desert.

Such development was often half-hearted, however. An attempt was made to irrigate portions of the Niger Delta for the purpose of growing cotton for export. A large amount of money was invested at first, but the results were mixed, and the French government soon lost interest.

Many European countries preferred to keep local leaders in place wherever and whenever possible, which was cheaper and easier than trying to install a foreign ruler. When the Europeans and the United States scrambled for Africa, they created new states. These new states did not correspond to the old kingdoms and empires that existed in pre-colonial times. Ruling them was going to be difficult for anybody. Though the new leaders were local, they answered ultimately to the colonial government. The British called this system indirect rule.

Local Resistance

Initially, Muslim leaders and scholars resisted colonialism. After France took control of Algiers, a local sheikh, Abd al-Qadir, organized a resistance in the countryside. People in the countryside were scattered and not necessarily friendly to one another. They came from different tribes and lived under their own political systems. Islam was one thing they all had in common. Abd al-Qadir appealed to their Muslim unity. "Let us therefore efface all the racial differences among true Muslims … and let us all have one armed hand raised against the enemy," he wrote in 1833. He resisted until 1847. Then, overwhelmed by the French's superior military, he surrendered and went into exile.

However, Islam continued to thrive under colonial rule, even expanding south. This was in part because Islam had such a long and successful presence in the region and in part because the European powers in many ways simply continued some of the projects that Muslim powers had begun. These goals included expanding trade, building up cities, and increasing literacy. Also, Europeans were more likely to work with local Muslim leaders than they were to work with local traditional leaders. At the same time, European colonial rulers were a secular challenge to Islam.

Education

Europeans brought with them European-style education. Though they offered several benefits, European schools were different and often conflicted with the established Islamic schools. In Algeria, the French tried to support two systems: the established Muslim schools, and new, secular schools designed to "make [locals] into decent, enlightened, prudent, hardworking men ... with the aim of improving their well-being, their hygiene, their agricultural practices and their industrial labor." In other colonies, like Tunisia and Morocco, the French put locals in charge of education. In still others, the French were in control, and education was entirely in French.

The End of the Colonial Era

In the 1930s, a new brand of Islam took hold in the Maghreb. A group of scholars who had trained in the Middle East formed the Association of Muslim Algerian Ulama (AUMA). It had, it claimed, "two noble

British Education and the Hausa Language

The British, in contrast to the more secular French, relied on religious orders to run their schools. At the same time, the British also worked with and supported local Muslim leaders. The British-run schools emphasized teaching in local languages. The British did not want a repeat of what had happened in India. There, they taught schools in English. When locals graduated from school, they spoke fluent English. They felt, not without reason, that this made them equal to other British citizens. Thus, they began demanding equal rights and protections. British schools in Africa taught grade school in local languages and introduced English only in the more advanced grades.

In Nigeria, the British supported the teaching of Hausa, a local language. The Hausa had been using the Arabic alphabet to write since the beginning of the nineteenth century. British administrators decided that if Hausa was going to be used to conduct local business, it should be written using the Roman alphabet (which is the alphabet used to write English). Locals resisted such a change at first because they feared that changing alphabets would mean abandoning Islam and encouraging Christianity. Despite this, the new version of Hausa, written in the Roman alphabet, was soon used to write popular historical novels. These included *Shaihu Umar*, the story of a boy kidnapped into slavery, taken into the desert, and returned home as an Islamic scholar. That is, in some ways, the story of trans-Saharan trade in a nutshell.

In present-day Timbuktu, mud-walled buildings are connected with electrical wires, as the city blends the old with the new.

aims: to restore the dignity of the Islamic religion and to restore the dignity of the Arabic language." At first, AUMA was not opposed to colonial rulers as much as they were opposed to the local Muslims

who cooperated with the colonial rulers. AUMA leaders thought Islam had become Westernized and pagan. From the Maghreb, different versions of the teaching spread west, and south. These teachings were often carried by students returning from the Middle East with a vision to restore and reinvigorate Islam.

This marked the beginning of the end of colonial rule. Religious and nationalist movements soon won independence for the nations of North and sub-Saharan Africa. In some cases securing independence required violence and war, but in some cases it was through a more peaceful transition of power. Debates over what constitutes an intellectually and culturally pristine version of Islam continue today. This conflict is at the root of many clashes that keep the region in turmoil. What was once a great highway, the center of the global economy, is now like it was prior to the advent of the trans-Saharan trade route: a dynamic, divided, conflicted mosaic of cultures.

Glossary

askia The ruler of the Songhai Empire.

banco Bricks and clay dried by the sun, used for building.

batin In Islam, the hidden meaning of something.

caravans Groups of people traveling together.

colonialism When a country takes control of another country for the purpose of gaining power and economic benefits.

cowrie shells A currency used in West Africa, traded along the trans-Saharan trade routes.

griots Traditional storytellers.

hajj A sacred journey to the Muslim holy city of Mecca. All Muslims are expected to make the trip at least once, if possible.

Islamicate A culture that is influenced by Islam.

jeli A public speaker who spoke for the king and told important stories.

koni A traditional West African lute, played like a guitar.

kora A traditional West African harp.

Koran The Muslim holy book.

Maghreb A region of North Africa, west of Egypt, bordering the Mediterranean Sea.

mansa The ruler of the Empire of Mali.

mosques Muslim places of worship.

nyamakalaw In Mande culture, the groups permitted to learn skills such as blacksmithing, music, and poetry.

Sahel The area on the southern edge of the Sahara where the land turns from desert to grassland.

secular Anything that is not religious.

Shia A smaller branch of Islam, whose adherents trace their authority back to the Prophet Muhammed's son-in-law.

sii Another title for the ruler of the Songhai Empire.

Sudan A region of the southern Sahara, stretching from western to eastern central Africa.

Sufism A form of Islam whose followers believe that holiness is achieved by withdrawing from the secular world.

Sunni The largest branch of Islam; Sunnis trace their authority back to the prophet Muhammed.

syncretism The blending of one religion with another.

toron Wooden poles used for building.

ulama A Muslim scholar.

zahir In Islam, the visible meaning of something.

Further Information

Books

Doak, Robin. *Empire of the Islamic World.* New York: Chelsea House, 2009.

Habeeb, William Mark. *Africa: Facts and Figures*. Jackson, TN: Mason Crest Publishers, 2012.

Van Voorst, Robert E. *An Anthology of World Scriptures*. Belmont, CA: Wadsworth Publishing Company, 2016.

Websites

African Kingdoms: West Africa
http://www.historyfiles.co.uk/KingListsAfrica/AfricaGhana.htm
Timelines, summaries, and biographical information are presented on this website hosted by the History Files.

Timbuktu
http://whc.unesco.org/en/list/119
Explore UNESCO's page devoted to the culture, history, and geography of the city of Timbuktu. This website features a photo gallery, interactive maps, and a video about how Timbuktu's monuments are "today under threat from desertification."

Tinariwen
http://tinariwen.com
Visit the official website of Tinariwen, a Grammy-winning group of Tuareg musicians. Tinariwen's website includes streaming music, videos of performances, and more.

The World of Islam
http://ngm.nationalgeographic.com/ngm/
data/2002/01/01/html/ft_20020101.5.html
National Geographic presents interesting facts, striking photographs, and suggestions for further reading about the religion of Islam.

Videos

"The Lost Libraries of Timbuktu." BBC, 2009.
This documentary tells the story of legendary Timbuktu and its long-hidden legacy of hundreds of thousands of ancient manuscripts.

"Sahara with Michael Palin." BBC, 2002.
A four-part series documenting a journey through Gibraltar, Morocco, Western Sahara, Mauritania, Senegal, Mali, Niger, Libya, Tunisia and Algeria.

Bibliography

Armstrong, Karen. *Fields of Blood: Religion and the History of Violence*. New York: Alfred A. Knopf, 2014.

———. *Muhammad: A Biography of the Prophet*. San Francisco: HarperSanFrancisco, 1992.

———. *Islam: A Short History*. New York: Modern Library, 2000.

Austen, Ralph. *Trans-Saharan Africa in World History*. Oxford, UK: Oxford University Press, 2010.

Benanav, Michael. *Men of Salt: Crossing the Sahara on the Caravan of White Gold*. Guilford, CT: The Lyons Press, 2006.

Conrad, David. *Great Empires of the Past: Empires of Medieval West Africa*. New York: Chelsea House Publishing: 2010.

De Villers, Marq, and Sheila Hirtle. *Timbuktu: The Sahara's Fabled City of Gold*. New York: Walker and Company, 2007.

———. *Sahara: The Extraordinary History of the World's Largest Desert*. New York: Walker and Company, 2002.

Gonzalez, Justo L. *The Story of Christianity: Volume 1*. San Francisco: HarperSanFrancisco, 1984.

Irvin, Dale T., and Scott W. Sundquist. *History of the World Christian Movement: Volume 1*. Maryknoll, NY: Orbis Books, 2003.

Keenan, Jeremy. *Tuareg: People of the Ahaggar*. London, UK: Sickle Moon Books, 2002.

Kenndy, Hugh. *The Court of the Caliphs: The Rise and Fall of Islam's Greatest Dynasty*. London, UK: Weidenfeld and Nicolson, 2004.

Kyrza, Frank T. *The Race for Timbuktu: In Search of Africa's City of Gold*. New York: Harper Collins, 2006.

Langewiesche, William. *Sahara Unveiled: A Journey Across the Desert*. New York: Vintage Books, 1996.

Marrozi, Justin. *South from Barbary: Along the Slave Routes of the Libyan Sahara*. New York: HarperCollins, 2001.

Newman, James L. *The Peopling of Africa: A Geographic Interpretation*. New Haven, CT: Yale University Press, 1995.

Pakenham, Thomas. *The Scramble for Africa*. New York: Random House, 1991.

Porch, Douglas. *The Conquest of the Sahara*. New York: International Publishing, 1986.

Sherrow, Victoria. *National Geographic Investigates Ancient Africa: Archaeology Unlocks Secrets of Africa's Past*. Washington, DC: National Geographic, 2007.

Smith, Huston. *The World's Religions*. San Francisco: HarperSanFrancisco, 1991.

Tayler, Jeffery. *Angry Wind: Through Muslim Black Africa by Truck, Bus, Boat, and Camel*. New York: Houghton Mifflin, 2005.

Index

Page numbers in **boldface** are illustrations. Entries in **boldface** are glossary terms.

Mansur, Abu Yusuf Ya'qub al-, 24
Mansur, Mulay Ahmad al-, 41, 51, 53–54
Marrakesh, 27, 54
Mecca, 17, 22–24, 42, **44**, 58
Mediterranean Sea, 4, 9, 14, 21, 27, 29, 33, 35, 78
merchants, 6, 20, 22, 25, 29–36, 38, 43, 45, 48–49, 51, 63–64, 67
Morocco, 9, 23–24, 27, 45–46, 51, 53–54, 59, 61, 76, 82
mosques, **63**, 64, 70, 72
Muhammad, Asika, 50–51
Muslim, 17–20, 22–25, 34, 38, 42-43, **44**, 49, **57**, 58-62, 64, 67-70, 73, 75, 81-84

Niger River, 4, 14, 31, 35, 48–49, 54
Nigeria, 75, 78, 83
Nmadi, 60
nomads, 6, 22, 25, 35, 39, 64, 68, 78
nyamakalaw, 67

oases, **8**, 10, 27, 30
Old Ghana, 22–23, 33, 67

panegyric, 68
Pasha, Jawar, 54

pilgrimage, 23–24, 42–43, 58, 61
poetry, 64–65, 67–69, 83
pulakuu, 69–70

Qadir, Abd al-, 81

Romans, 14, 19

Sahel, 9, 11, 20, 31, 47, 68
Sahili, Abu Ishaq al-, 44
salt, 13, 24–25, 29–31, **29**, 33–35, 38, 52, 80
Sanhaja, 7, 22
scholars, 22, 49, 59, 62, 64, 67–69, 73, 81–83
secular, 61, 64, 69, 82–83
Senegal, 22
Senegal River, 31
Shia, 59–60
sii, 49–50
slaves, 13, 18, 25, 29–30, 32–35, 38, 42–43, 54
Songhai, 7, 24–25, 41, 48–51, 53–55
Soninke, 7, 67
Sorko, 48
Spain, 18–19, 24, 33, 46, 54, 57, 60
Sudan, 9, 11, 13, 27, 57, 65, 67–68, 75, 78–79
Sufism, 61–62
Sufris, 20
Sunni, 59
syncretism, 61

About the Author

Matt Lang was raised in western Pennsylvania. He went to college in Erie, Pennsylvania, transferred to the College of Wooster, and in time, moved to Chicago, where he now lives in an intentional community with many other people, including his wife and daughter.

Lang is the author of *The Giraffe's Mustache: A Storybook You Can Color*, *McKean County and Other Stories*, and *Fernweh*.